not a story

CRPD

ISBN: 978-1981892051

ISBN-13: 1981892052

I don't want to tell you a narrative
I want to speak life
through wide open joyful mouths
and tight-lipped sobs
I want to grit my teeth
and bite my tongue
and pray at the edge
of holy majesty
I am not here to tell you a story
I am here

This is not a story.

This is a collection of moments lived and loosely captured.
Invited, cried, fought, loved and a thousand other things
as life's moments are.

I invite you into Living.

ACKNOWLEDGMENTS

This collection as an extension of my life is only possible
through the interconnected world we are woven into.

I am deeply grateful to every being and person who has touched
my life, known and unknown.

To my family, every single piece of it.
How lucky I have been to have you.

To the community of Vista Yoga, Marti and Marty,
thank you for creating a space
to explore life with more awareness.
It has made my life what it is and will be.

A deep thank you to Carroll who has been a powerful spark of
inspiration and bliss in life's poetry.

I am so deliciously
not myself
terrifying inseparable
from
action
experience
you
witness to
thin mist that dances
a story of shadows
through backlit eyes
every piece and layer
undone
swept up and out of the way
all of life
living itself

Rain is pouring down
        with such force

    droplets are pushed back up
      splashing away
          from the ground
             they long to absorb
                  into

      A string of small mirrors
    (placed to catch the shimmer of the sun)
      are caught now in the wind

        swinging wildly
     Back
   and
     forth
   a pendulum
 losing control
      into
        the uneven fearful jarring
     of thunder

     a loud boom
     bright light
     fill the sky
the downpour pauses in the fleeting moment of such

     Brilliance

on instinct
      the storm returns to fervor
mirrors no longer shifting
I feel the cool breeze of change
  Remembering
     Reflections of a stillpoint

My heart feels
as small as a speck of dust
clinging
to a maple seed
and to a hope
of finding meaning
there
more than with the rest of the ground

dreaming of bright red leaves
dancing through the rough life wind
strong and tall and powerfully
FREE!

While silently staying safe
and shelled
and small

Scared
(as hell to)

Break open
and find there is
nothing inside me
able to grow

The moon flower grows
through sticky styrofoam shards
scattered around the overflowing dumpster
unplanted
overlooked
underwatered

Illuminated
by a blinding fluorescent flood light

It sends
a single trumpeting bloom
into the still
sleeping morning
limp and browning
remains
of other night's glory
hang around her
curtains
for her short and unanxious performance

She blooms.
into one woman's soul
in the waning moments
of a dark dark night

sometimes
    I feel confident
    tearing into the direction life has chosen for me
    savoring every ripening strawberry
    reaching
    full and red and perfect
        FREE
    from concerns for the path ahead
        thrown open
    to the joy around
        this
sometimes
    I am so scared
    I pray for life to unlive me
    to remove the small me
        Away
    from the world
        Leaving
    only the vast being
    needing no assurances
    understanding and living
        Truth
sometimes
    the doubts fluttering by like hummingbirds
    barely blurring the edges
    of my mind's
    wide open
    view of a beautiful morning

sometimes
    I feel I have no choice
    at all
        Falling
    into the flow
    that drags me
    Fast, Slow, Rough, and easy
    rubbed raw
    where I have bound myself
    to familiar shores
    undertow waiting to pull me
    in a direction
    that could seem like forward
    if I can let go
sometimes
    it is not the next step
    I Fear
    it is the unknown hundreds
    that could follow
sometimes
    I wonder
    what it could be
    to worry in the direction of love
    to open my heart
    wider at every anxious crack
    to seek the joy that seeks me
    to cry and laugh and jump
    in the faith
    that this is all
    Living

Have you ever thought this burning
is supposed to be

The flames were meant to char
your edges and spread
across your skin
you were designed to speak
in forks and dagger
consuming
what you insist to push away

Did you ever imagine in the ashy piles
of your pain
there would be a jewel
faceted just enough to reflect it all

well of course not,
because you know better and more
and faster the desire for the
burning to stop!

but Do not hurry
through this supposed destruction

Breathe and watch the dance
what truth do the flickering shadows hold

Gather around you
all the people
that speak
their truth
so imperfectly
            (as humans do)
and when their pointed light upsets your foundation
dig down into the places they point to
where the porch slopes downward and
        the siding has rotted away
reveal the parts of you trapped
        against the houses you have built
unable to grow
bleed the roots where they have tangled
        over themselves
    leaching the most precious of your wells
when the pain settles
watch your spirit run again
toward deeper water

When most will say the easy
    let the garden run dry
    rather than changing
    any pattern long knotted & broken
draw close those
        who speak the storm
and bring new rain to hard and thirsty roots

Death is a deniable reality
whole lives seem to persist on ability to deny it

Deny this moment
   is as important as the ones
   that come later
   or have already passed
more maybe
     that this moment is all there is

                          To Be

Death reminds us
in flashes of unbearable grief
that we are doomed to lose
the most precious of life's gifts
Not most likely, not probably
but with a certainty we cannot accept
Except in overwhelming flashes
that blind us from the lies of our lives
and let us see the truth of living
the perfect impermanence
An unreasonable gift

Death's desolation
peaks at the edge of a wide arc
swinging back to the (potential) joy
of all that is
not death

Let us not forget the joy
    the breathes being into this life
Let us not forget the loss
    of all that is

I have returned to the secret bench
    and the sweet energy you have left me
It is a break in my first day and I feel
    a thousand things I haven't decided on yet
    and I feel your voice in the high Sante Fe breeze

"How do you do it?" I ask you

you answer, not in words.
                    I don't know

In a lot of ways disruption from the routine is jarring
It gives us a view into the larger part of our lives

This time I feel I am small
    I am a tiny
        tiny
              infinite being

The beautiful thing is I don't have
    to live this world's dharma
or even another being's dharma
    to be the truth of this world

I simply have to make way
           and allow

Unexpectedly
I look up
to see
your smile
perfect
as it has been for as long as
I have known you

What could be more beautiful
than the upturned edges of
your eyes

brown with golden rays

suns

They, like you,
seem so unreal
and the reason for reality

Today I want the world
to satisfy me
        differently
hhh...hippo hop is closed
and I am left kicking
        on the ground
even the unconditional
love of my Yaya not enough
not even present in my
        miserable disappointment

    Like an old man yelling
out in his sleep
        fighting every face
and force that creates discord
        for his world

    I cry out at the illusion
sinking deeper into the veils of myself

...the slow drop of practice
    acknowledgement and movement
promises change
            one sip at a time

Seek the way
through the waves that cascade the mind
sucking us under
into the rolling currents
of thought and need and anger
disguised as urgency for understanding

Release into the undertow
sink deeper than the smallest bubble
                        of thought
and feel in the vast dark ocean
        the depth of you
the depth of us

If we have to go through the vrittis
I am not sure we'll get anywhere at all

Thank you for trusting me
        the universe sighs
at the edge of a choice
that left life frozen in
   confusion and fear

            The other edge is still
touching those dark places
                        & the rest of infinity

Life
must seem glorious
or
idiotic
to the dead

^{and} I am sad
^{and} I don't hate
sadness

I just don't know
what to do

Sitting in the back seat
    of a comindeered car
the self-declared spiritualist
in stained faded ochre cut-edged sweats
looks into the rearview mirror
    past me

        "All I know is my feelings don't matter."

A lifetime of inquiry in a
single phrase

Sri Sri Sri Guru
        fucked-up Steve Hamby

He says my poems speak the best
when they come from a place of nothing

So if I lust or desire or (FORBID) my god-given ego craves
to write
then will they not find me?

Of course not, my love
the whole world wants to share its greatest secrets with you

Birth
of a dragonfly or flower or perfectly expressive line
is as mysterious as finding home in everyday
self after self

We aren't meant to know
but we can be ready, open to wanting
impassioned pen in hand

Patient Transformation

A large green dragonfly
appears at rest
on an old rocking chair
translucent wings outstretched
the points of a star
expanding

the dead hollow husk of him
still clings to where he started
a different being
shell trapped
      and I, *a world of not understanding*

long wet white wings heavy in the still air

            Stillness
                        maintained through
                        the careless rushing of other life
            harded his wings
      into something barely separate
      from the all around him

power vibrates through his dazzling new self
ready to fly before the heavy rain comes

like flashes it comes to me

                          gate

the gone and here both
   and you cannot hold
it
  though you cup your hands
in on all sides
      and hum softly sacred
          melodies
even though my hands
      are empty
     I am here

            pāragate

When I am dead
      Write to me
Tell all your worries
    Let me take them home
    Heart open to even the
      smallest
    Care of sorrow or joy
Sit on my grave
        in sunshine
            or shade
                or rain
Free your questions
    as loud or as soft as they want to fly
Answer will come
    as a whisper
    in the deep vibrations of your heart
    echoing truths
    I cannot yet understand
Speak to me
    All your secrets
      I will love you
  As all the dead love all the living
      At peace
    not not waiting to
  welcome you into the ground

Do you think the admired fig tree
left seemingly untouched
    to be
        in effulgent space
                + sun
loves
    the darkness just as much?

Budding spring and bloom,
    laden fruit and now
        so unexpectedly
    snow
     it holds it all

The hand of the gardener
slides the potted earth
further into the heat of the day
against the supposed order
others have tried to create
in 'their' corner
of the universe

Out

from the shadow of the overgrown privet
the hibiscus can bloom
More &
More Powerfully

Unfurling
Blood red
Bud and Blossom
upward
into the white sky

Opening to
all the world
Brilliance, Potential

There
Walked Past
Seen

When
night falls
each unopened petal follows
to darken
to drop
an unmindful push
sends an unremarked plant
back
growing hope and faith
for the gardener's love
to drag a willing bloom
out
again and again

"Fuck Them"
A phrase smooth from the rolling
   Falls off the tongue
      Occupying the space between
                my teeth

A practiced response
   to the (scenario or opinion that seems)
        impossibly ignorant and immovable
Another brick in the wall laid
          "Fuck Them"

              Separation
(My) reaction is the offence

              Samskara

Truth floats in a question
        "Why
          do you have to go
             there?"
             (where we all stand
             not looking in
             each others' eyes)

Begging me to understand
        (not know)
What it would be to include
          (them)
              (their)experience
              (their)(re)action
              (their)(fuck you!)
        all of it held
           closer than the whys

The educator
    eyes as black as a magpie's
seizes the free air
to show his newest feather of information
preened into his elaborate mask
    new crumb and old trash
    piled on together
    displayed as treasure to anyone
    whose eyes pass
        (so they will pass him
          so he will not have to see past himself)
I do not trust a blackbird that mocks
    the owl's song
I want to syphon each mimicked melody
    from that mind
clear away the shiny horde
    with truths that explode
        (when thought
         not thought through)
lighting the data bobbles
until every part of the self is on fire
thick protective layers
        (fear, denial, pain, history, samskara)
Dancing in flames
Bare soul
at last
illuminated

What is your contribution to the
        suffering
When you believe their change
        is hard?
Does a bitter tasting story
        sweeten with your sympathy?

I have no answer for your beliefs
            nor reasoned objections

Speak the world of choice
        not samskara
then what stories would you hear?

No one can make you wrong
          they can think it
          they can say it
    but you are you no other way

               glorious, free
            made of mistakes
                        and successes
          (some of which overlap)

let's sing to today and tomorrow
          and the next day
let's hold our own heart
               towards the sun,
                    honoring it all

Between the town of my birth
     and the country of my raising

I stopped
to share a few moments
     with an old friend
I climbed along the gold and green
     grassy hill, weaving between 200-
     year old oaks and headstones
Until I spotted the family place
     of my dear Emily
Entering through the unlocked gate
I placed a single blue delphinium

Two young people left
     having never really entered
Taking their cold drinks and pictures
Leaving a ring of condensation
                    on Lavinia's grave
Joking of people who sit on dead people

Silly boy, as if dead people are some other
          type of people
we are not

What does ignorance create in this world?
                    truth?
We see only the outcome of their mixture

Settled, beneath the old flat leaf conifer
(which must at least partially be a Dickenson)
I ask Emily the questions on my heart
Speaking to whatever ears can listen,

                                    my own?
The world and emily whisper through me
Every person alive (in spirit or genetic code)
Every generation (back and back and back)
My personality a byproduct of their replication

Who is to say who I am?
Who is to say who I am not?

Every dead person sitting on
        every dead person's grave
Plus one,
        not yet in the ground

There is no need to feel guilty
    for happiness,
and by extension there is no need
        to feel guilt for doing what makes
    you happy
Happiness is such a precious jewel
    in the world
Spread your arms and let it in
there are few things as worthy
        to open to

What is
our white elephant?
The thing
we can point to and say
I want that
no matter what the cost
to someone or some other thing
not yet manifest

Can we lean into desire
with dice waiting
for some other hand
to roll
and take
their turn
to say with echoed gusto

"I want! I want!"

to not fear desire or loss
that is the game
choose well the rounds worth playing
choose well the gifts worth playing for

Sometimes
the separation
between us
Shimmers
like a crystal
with a power to refine and reflect
all the ways I love you

The way you see
the world
approach it
parts you fear
and embrace
developing
understanding
love
when I sit across the table from you
space grows and does not exist
It almost brings me to tears
how beautiful you are

Tell me what words to
write to make me feel whole
what relationships to cultivate
or turn away from

I need darkness
slipping into the mud
slipping out of my clothes
piece by piece
starting with anything
        I think
        I know
and then any other piece
            of story or knowledge
        I take a deep breath
before I go under
        then another

12:15pm North Passenger Drop-off
Hartsfield-Jackson International Airport

What a perfect place
to rush! The airport
another few dozen moments
that need not be lived;
                            slowly

hurry! hurry!
    to your place
        to your people
don't be here
    alone and in transition
    destination is the sweetness of life
when in doubt
        be where you are going
not where you are in the going too

I wonder
if I would love
to be
in a busy, small New England town
just at the winter's edge of fall
the smell of not-yet frost
and firey leaves
floating through the bright
white-grey sky

People
walk slowly
unburdened
by the slippage
of time

I imagine Charles Herr
enjoyed this corner
of Ferry and S Main

Gone and still
the enshrined black bench,
thoughtful peace,
and unbound day
along the Delaware River

What a selfish thing is life!
   to be driven by the desires
     of the apparently limited

When the universe itself grows
   with every human heart
beat outward in every direction
    even those
we cannot possibly know

What can be
       known
       seen
       felt
       understood
       experienced
         is limited
     by how we limit ourselves
   what awe are we allowed to have
    within our boundaries

Boundaries like
    dotted lines
        through the infinite

      I would rather be
         unbounded

     floating without anchor
     in the limitless

What Changes
the world or my heart
when I am unburdened
by time

It seems to even shift the wind,
people's foot falls

Perhaps it is the most
luxurious decadent delicacy
—time

Good company and warm love
right beside it as
the most delicious pieces
of an abundant world

A sea of sky the
clouds roll over each other like the
latest of evening tides
smooth and lightly moving out

I am moving in and
in so fast it all seems to reach
endlessly behind the hot wake of my open wings

Can you imagine far above
birds flying, just a simple
human
                going home

What a treasure
to take the gift
of practice
with me
in every step
along the wide river

Watching the near white sky
reflected
in the gliding water

To have the luxury of time
and the luxury of presence in it

Thank you!

Thank you!

Completion
is not written
a chiseled list of:
- time spent
- goals achieved
- goods accumulated

Done
is the full feeling in your soul
when the world seems to hold,
even for just a few seconds,

enough

We stepped out together
into the darkness
door shut behind us
and he said *this way*
the way opposite all familiarity and movement

I questioned
        but chose to trust
as he led me toward the forest in the cold rain

            "Have you ever been here"

We crawled through the gate
        with just enough room to stand
in the wall-less shelter
        I pulled him against me
                warmth in the cold dark

I could see every drop of beauty
        that was offered to me
enjoying the view so as he kissed me
                            or I him

What a beautiful solitude
your companionship has
brought me

My mind is soaked
with the ocean

In wonder
Where will I stand
and see to grow this
expanding view

In all the words of objection
I have screamed and whispered
I never realized their cries
    were for my soul

    "Don't make me less free."

    "Do not be less free."

Garuḍāsana

So many parts of me
twisted into knots until I have no
          idea what order
        I should be in

I want to close my eyes and give in
to being helplessly bound

I keep them
        open and focused

Drawing in,
        I will fly again

At the boundary is where
we are broken down
like beaches on islands so
small in a vast ocean
the edges of us wear away
until even our driest sand is in
the sea, in + out and in + out
the churning bringing us
closer to boundlessness

I am grateful for the still water after a long day of storms
that trap me within
the shell of myself
turned to thought and
distraction

I go out and almost
tricking myself I run
for the shore
paddle in hand to slip along the foggy surface

Alone
but for the million other parts of
myself

The cove's shades of darkness usher me still
And I turn to see a brilliant moon
In its fullness there is no thought that I am anything
other
lack absent

It seemed to be pulled across the sky by some great rig
and I was drifting too
though I had stopped pushing myself along

thank you

Watch all the others look in
but not stay
        never stay
until they do
        some barely make it
past the threshold
                new and old alike
        I guess it matters
where on the journey
you meet them and what they are
expecting
what they don't see
                its all apart
of the view

It is fun to be at an end
and watch everyone turn
around
        looking up for one moment
then going back out
                when you are here
every place is mesmerizing
    and is anywhere else

What a wonder
is loneliness
Could it be freedom?
if we embrace
what we resist
sink down, drink in
the truth in our apparent separation
the hope of embracing desperation
seeing ourselves
barely and completely
as we are
alone

free
of trying
to be

anything

in any one's eyes

Tell me again that I am going to die
Again and again
Never let me forget
Each moment of bliss
Is precious and fleeting
Every understanding
Every meeting of hearts
Lasts just as long as thought flickers

That while longing is eternal
so is peace
presence
this moment

the whole of us
all pieces
all places
all beings
will return to the womb of the universe
and will be

Through the narrowest exit of an overgrown cove
two ducks mated

He took her black neck feathers in his yellow bill
and dunked her under the water with the weight of himself

Unafraid, they looked at me
Rising up with great flaps of his powerful white wings
Shaking of the wet

I passed, still
captivated by the quick union

This is life
      they seemed to say to me
settling back into their slow separateness
      as if there was
not a single thought to the contrary

It is life's nature to crave knowledge _{as if}
    it can help know what is beyond understanding

            to crave power _{as if}
    it can control what is beyond control

            to crave ownership _{as if}
    anything is beyond being lost
                    even our self

All samskara, all self
    is built on a shifting coastline of here and gone
the only freedom from the gain and loss
    Embracing
the immense vulnerability
        Look at the samskara
that seek
        us to feel safe
            binding us to mirages
                of security

Let go of their false truths now
                (or let them rip from you in death)
            opening to the magnificence of the world
            (from the poor soft squishy stupid scared
            self-centered uncontrolled place you stand)
                Grounded on a spinning earth
                looking out into wonderment

I think I saw
      the edge
        of Avedya
In the apparent space
        between
        two-human beings
            desperately confused
            wanting
without looking   for the answer
        to the truth
            of the asking question(s)
seeking in the night
            to know
circling past   the bright sky
        the still
            rocky ridge
of understanding
Above a racing highway
    bowing their eyes over
                their world's edge
Holding out two fingers and squinting
to measure   the distance between
          each   ———   other
          "that far"
That far from leaping in any direction
    That far from a certain dying
        That far from themselves
            forgetting
                the feeling
                    of
            not-not being

together
alive and still

Let us take a good hard look at the self
    the mask over the mirror
        the personality, the ego
            the vehicle to get from and cope with
          our experience of the world

Is it straight forward
    to say
        the self is self-ish
at best seeing the hazy outline of its bias
    compensating in action what it cannot compensate for
              in existence
at worst by samskara
    of knowledge, of power, of ownership
    the self-ishness grows as large as the self
            larger
        ego, entitlement, arrogance
      Always acting from a place of self(ish)
        The nature of its being

Do you imagine the moon thinks
    of its tides
or the lovers of this world
    gazing up in wonderment

Does the sun know
    its imperfect burning
    shines bright white upon reflection
    or churns life into being

Do you feel all the ways
    you slip and slide
    between the planes of this existence

burning and pulling
        and reflecting

Who knows what light
    your moons soften
  and what life
    your tides churn

There is a healing power
in a morning with you
Wakening presented
in such delicious presence
that slippery resistances long to melt
the Mask
reforming itself new
New light
brings apparent form to the darkness
I wonder
as you insist on being
if the whole worked world
could be healed
drinking half-a-cup of
            Rich, Sweet, Bitter
and watch the sunrise
            of a dear earnest soul
      over Atlanta

Home is not the place we are from but the place we seek
Found between lovers, friends, heartbeats,
lines of a perfect poem,
a favorite smell,
a summer breeze,
the reflection of sunlight on a rippling pond,
the cricketing of a bird call

Home is a space larger than
any place or person or moment and
found inside them all

If we can just be still long enough to
feel byond the gap

We are so easily wounded
A single thought aimed at the soft spots of our hearts
    Triggers a downward spiral of whispers
        Telling us to tighten muscles around those bruises
        To close off, to guard
    Barking at every imperfect being that dares get too close
    Digging at ourselves for being so stupid as to openly let
        them
Like a dog locked in a kennel
                                        our heart sits longing
        to explore, to play, to share, to love
        to be explored, to be touched, to be loved

While our mind and body are fitted to work in the world

Setting yourself free
    Means embracing the cuts and bruises
        People are scared and stupid and arrogant and reckless
        Hiding behind a barbed wire gate thay do not realize is
unlocked
            (Do not forget
            your own hands have twisted
            many links
            with mindless trespass)
cuts heal, trespasses mend
(and if we let them)
hearts will love of their own true nature
            Focus on that sense of love
(through the stinging voices of fear, doubt, misunderstanding)
            Follow it past the thinnest of shadows
                to the vast open steppe of Love
                Invite the whole world out with you

After the wisdom knowledge
    you must step along the path
        unlearning, unknowing
until being is left
    as pure as the first drop of
water from an open sky
          wonderment returns
like a 3-year-old naming all
      the world with his fingers and toes

A beautiful night
Layers of blue sit on top of each other
illuminated by crispy bright stars
in the dry desert sky

I hear the first human voices
in a chorus of flowing water and cooing birds

half wants

You would probably be reading a poem
right now

If someone cared about you
like they did
in the now yesterday imagination
and like drops of water
through luminous hands
over dirty feet
its words would slip away
the grime of wrong and right
into being
as softly as
answered prayers
whispered into silence

I am caught in gratefulness
      and greed
like the fly in
      the desirous net of a spider
cast wide

          Does want create gratefulness?
             no, only greed
satisfaction is a lie

          I am held so completely
          I want more + more
      though I have been offered nothing
        but abundance

Perhaps it is the yogi's practicing
      to be the world
abundant and unasking

    What if I offered myself
      the truth
the space to be with and without

Not a rejection or an impulse wanting
I love what comes. I love what goes.

pull me pull me this way
and that and I flit
to it like a kite
but so desperately I
yearn for my wings to
flap their own rhythm
and float on a heart
longed updraft

My Life, My Muses, and
My Own

Down in the deep dark
sadness. I sit
and wail, so soft
it hurts my heart
and my throat
I try to let it
be heard
and hands in my heart
the bloody thing
        whispers
'No one can hear you'

I can hear you

I am all-right
    just in the process of living
the tearing down and
    rebuilding of my heart
  takes a lot of tears

    there is no blueprint
for freedom
    just a feeling
we choose with each breath
        and lose just as much

live how you can darling
    and be <u>alive</u>
            your heart is the world
hold it close

Be vigilant of each sliver of righteousness
      (so easily recognized when it is stuck
         in another's flesh)

It grows along the veins of your being
      like a cut of kudzu
         wrapping you in tendrils
and sending roots where your nastiest
                        soot + grime touch the air
      wide leaves unfurl to the light you worship
leaving only darkness
         for what you were meant to grow

I think perhaps the greatest gift is

                                    'got it'

understood and let
be, there is no
need to defend
because it is not my voices
yelling in your ear

And though you may
not be able to understand
you need not
be right or wrong

I suppose if you want
    a reaction
you'll have to have it
        yourself

I do not want to be bound to you

I want to hold your hand free
    from all the knotted
fears and lies that hold arms back
    away from what they yearn to
                Reach for

I do not want a new rope
    (I love many enough to struggle
  already)

I want the freedom to hold on
            and let go

Here's to the being workers
the open uppers, the tearer downers

They are the rebuilders
         when first there must be demolition

Do I need a simple shift in piping
         or a complete leveling
I do not know but I
              (or Isvara)
         have put this self in line for the wrecking
   ball, as I feed and water my being
not-not ready for impact

It is quite nice to love
some being or doing
that does not match with
the societal expectations
of you(r identity)

So when you feel that
            deep
            heart-whole
            beyond the understanding
Appreciation

and the world
(and a part within your mind)
tries to tell you
"It is not OK."

you will question
all the ideas
the world and your mind
insist upon

Realizing
limits are just air
that bars were talked into

There is no freedom left to fear

Oh breathe!

What kind of thing am I
hopping along the ground
and sky, in and out of lines defined
into simply here

surrounded by the movement
neither expanding or contracting

being

You can buy me.
I would gladly sell
my actions to you

When the list of what
I would do
(for money)
is the same as what
I would do
(for free)

Money is liquid
unbinding energy

flowing through being
leaving behind
only the taste
of pure conjuration

manifestation
of real dreams
in an imaginary world

It is a convenient lie
    that I am not
        living my dharma
                She says across a cup of tea
                never not shared

I am here
    I have to be
    here
            this is all Dharma

In the darkness
        just before sunrise
You sit on the edge
        of where we have been
        lying
In the appearance
    of difference
--Form and Veil--
    We are both
        seeing
        the same

Captured
by the lure
of unfolding petals
The Flower Thief
Reaches
into the knee-high branches
of a Magnolia
SNAP
the bloom just perfect
to be
tasted by the long
-ing tongues
of two *Whirling* butterflies
GREEDY
to taste everything
and everything
of each other

Race + Grasp
for the
there + there
in the haze making fog
You miss
the ocean at your feet
close enough
you're already touching

A very blue bird calls shrilly
    from the lowest arms of a desert bush
he bobs; and waits;
        and flys
    to the top of the zendo
          hopping along its nailless roof
where the three young residents
          of days
listen to a longing soulful song
      "we finally we finally won"
    young hearts going for this life
      free spirits or still in this weave tight
does it matter?   Live! for the life of you
          Live!

In the afternoon shadows
    two birds take the low place
near the bubbling water of this oasis

I will eat the moon
until I am full and golden
the world is dark blue and grey
I will paint it outside of color

When our souls touch
I will feed light
simply by reaching
out and asking they will
think its mine
though it is reflected from every other
shining place
        in the universe

Quietness

You listened
            to me read the poetic lines
    that vibrated your space in my being
and you shared with me
        'we had shared these words
    on the day I washed your feet'

        I was there exhausted
                    holding your hand
            for the first time
            breathing in
    your nervous excitement
                    and my own

        I was lying face down
                    on smooth granite
    the cool lake water dripping
                from your hands
    to the souls
            of my feet
                    deeply relaxed
in the touch of your not yet touching

        I was at the other end
        of a distant connection
    longing for you and to never be separate from you
        knowing there is no
                    and never was
            separation

What would I like to teach tonight?
Maybe that life is too precious to spend
on doing and not at all
on being

      When am I supposed to be present?
        on everyone else's schedule

I danced with the storm last night
tip toes and pirouettes
on long slick stones
flashes of night
after a long dark day
(of tasks at hands
and works to be done)
oh and how the world kissed me!
all over, fifty times at once!
and how much love and longing I felt
for her too
as I blew her a single kiss
and came inside
dry and warm and health
another day

almost how
a slip and twirl
of a perfect beautiful dance
and all of me given
to that storm
if the frozen parts of me would sway
to the boom of thunder

People seem to believe the trick
to becoming a writer is to
write. It is to live.

The first and truest
art is life. All others must
rest within its strokes

Rob yourself of each moments truth
and all you are left with
is a series of lies, lived sequentially
like pictures in someone else's memory book

What holds you from being
now

nothing
more than every voice that isn't yours
let those voices still and settle
with your own
SPEEK
every word and action
from the truthful core of
your living

Moved around
at others' whim and wind
and by none of it
simply placed, right
in the perfect spot for
the unhurried unfolding
of the universe

stolen moments
rushed in + out of
always trying to break
away into the nothing
we are

A young boy
pees on a tree
while a woman holds
his ice cream

The shock of unhidden humanity
animalistic normalcy, life
when the rest of the world
hurries in boxes
to other boxes
and I sit
in the sun

Now my lovers of the world
Now is the time to be warriors of that love
Love yourself fiercely
Love your neighbor fiercely
Love your brothers and your sisters and Humans fiercely

Let your heart weep, but not more than it needs to

Your heart needs you
Your world needs you, love warrior

I hear each wind
as if it could be him
Beloved telling me he can
find a place to understand
                    (not me or him)
something beyond that

What guides the pattern
            of leaves and ants
            of sunrises and chickens
            of love and sorrow
all alive at the base of my being

                    I wonder which
                    will come forward
                    Hope
                    for a whisper
                    of that unknowing place

What gratitude I feel after
the lessons the universe held for me
this morning

The gift of emotional disturbance
the frustration of a cat
scratching at a locked door
going back again
and again
because he is not in control of it

There is a deep place within
me
where I do not feel worthy
to simply be me

What if no one's thoughts mattered
not even my own

Is the aim
to make it through
the times of being a (shitty) human
where in front of all the joy there
seems to be
this great
uncomfortable
a universal arthritis
that dampens even the most beautiful
compressing the space between every cell
swelling seams between subtle souls

Do we make it though
are we made through it

Is there even a through
or is the place to be
here
in the mud
allowing, releasing, loving
being
until the beams of morning sunlight
fall through the towering canopy
and
illuminate

You can give someone the stars
with a whisper
touching every inch of
earth and sky
with your tongue
a heart beats the time
of potentiality
who knows
what moons it will become
this moment
the whole-universe
breathes
and
sighs
all that is
and is to is
and is to is to is

All the things people don't want
                         to hear
are written across my heart

As if I should hide away
from my truth
for the comfort of others

What if I made no more
excuses for my being and
                <u>was</u>

Allowing for all
              my faults and feelings
         and theirs
as if they all had value

Vīrabhadrāsana I

I forgot I could
stand
          be here

I forgot
     but my body remembers
my being remembers

Sometimes the cave calls me
Sometimes the sun
                    who's to argue
the dark depths of our mind-less
being is more urgent
                    than the light
        of this world?

A full orange moon
seemed to spread the sky
yesterday as we drove
separate and together
what a wonder!
for only $36

Today
        the price
            for only a single pot of coffee
                        was all of my joy
                if even for a few moments
                together and separate
                too high a price

So easily forgotten
which way to turn my heart
to live under the full sky

In the smoke of confusion
it is easy to hate
the self
to feel deserving
of every feared and desired
punishment
that a sinful mind could think

In that shadow
of the holy
condemnation
as you pass each crucifying nail
through
the narrow bones
of a fragile and fleeting
human soul

Love Yourself

and if all you find within
is your darkness
Believe there is a light
of understanding
so vast, so brilliant, so beyond
that it cannot help but Love You

I see pain on my sister's face
    lying like a new life on her side
            after practice

I want to whisper
                that is my pain too
but she already knows
        we all already know

Sandia Mountain

Heavy rain, lightning, high winds
grey, grey past the first row
of trees with hail bouncing
off heads and decks and
sleeves which is almost
preferable to the heavy round
drops as big as marbles
soaking down into all the layers of your skull
to chill you
in the hottest Summer days in New Mexico
the temperature drops + drops
the humans are noisy in
their excitement to reach the top

I don't know who we are
Do I need to know?
or in the quick moments
we are blessed to share can I
feel my way
to not understanding

You can do little more than be
baptized in the fight of curning
waters before you are spit
back out onto shore

Wet, Cold, and Fearful
and yet the roar and color
calls me close to
                    Mother Ocean

As a contribution to you
    take a deep breath in
    hand that person a flower
as if they were your most deeply loved
    and bow to all the gifts they have given you

        Release
        count...2...3
        Repeat

            until it doesn't matter
where their mind and heart are this morning
    only you are there
      underneath the personalities that bind us to
the actions of this world
      Simply the being

            together

Most times
my life is expansive
licking the sweet shining joy
Grace
leaks out between every beat of my heart
Love and appreciation for the world, for my life
seeps between the cells of my body
Holding me
together
(like glue)
and illuminate
(any possible dislike of)
this precious moment
gifted
to me

Sometimes
like a human
I am
Overwhelmed
by an accumulation, overlooked or ignored
of relationships, of responsibilities, of limitations
expectations and emotions asked
of my dear human
by life or by my own self

Small drops
that normally slide down the sides of me
Back to the earth
returning
to
the illusion that created them
evaporating
in practice and grace

Stuck
the waters stagnate
growing sadness and anger and others
almost impossible to see in the darkness
deep
enough to flood the heart

An offending drop
stone heavy
skips along the still surface
until it sinks
daring to disturb the long-built sludge
splashing drops of the mire
over the pitiful human head
tasting of bitter anger
resting on a melancholy tongue

on my luckiest days
I can remember I am breathing
that unchanging current
guides me
through the temporary
To anxiously paddle
towards a memory
of happiness
when caught
in the spiral
of a drain
breaking free
its stopper
leads me only to idle

Pull in the oars
Breathe
let the tide carry
the human out
to Peace again

I sip you like a sun tea
left in this life to brew
beside the Louisiana sun that grew
you and all the bitter spirits
you had to taste

A guru in the mud
                    not about it
uncomfortable and blooming

How can we be together? It seems the
longer we face each-other the less we
exist dissolving the edges of ourselves
into the immensity of the being that
surrounds us...shhh...darling...it is
the morning the sun and I rise together
always having been we whisper
to each other of what our being
is like   burning the beings - past and
future to propel our shapes and those around
our shapes while being moved by unseen
engines through this dance

        Our biggest trespass
                        is holding on
        It is almost as if it is
                        our only one

The mind desires understanding
so frantically
　　　　that it is willing
　　to believe a known lie

　　　　　　But
　　　　　　　we get to create
　　　　　　　　the space
　　　　　　　　for ourselves in this world

　Don't be in a hurry and push
　through
　　　　　　　　　　　just be
in the moment
　　　　in your not-not centered
　　it is the way of this world

　　　　　　　I could have you live in your assumptions
　　　　　　　but I want to live authentically

The universe is always asking us to keep expanding

This is not completion
            it is complete...
whole and unending
        every direction and
                none—eternity

I do not rest in infinity
    I laugh and skip
    and slip and sigh

I am grateful for this
        expanse and for this
        narrowness

Let us stop and just stop
        and watch the sunset together

Caroline Dunham
is being;
creating herself
and the practice of yoga
in Atlanta, GA.

You can contact Caroline
at crpdfree@gmail.com.

Made in the USA
Columbia, SC
05 February 2018